The Universe

The Earth

Anne Welsbacher

ABDO & Daughters

Published by Abdo & Daughters, 4940 Viking Drive, Suite 622, Edina, Minnesota 55435.

Copyright © 1997 by Abdo Consulting Group, Inc., Pentagon Tower, P.O. Box 36036, Minneapolis, Minnesota 55435 USA. International copyrights reserved in all countries. No part of this book may be reproduced in any form without written permission from the publisher.

Printed in the United States.

Cover and Interior Photo credits: Peter Arnold, Inc.
Illustrations: Ben Dann Lander
Edited by Bob Italia

Library of Congress Cataloging-in-Publication Data

Welsbacher, Anne, 1955-
The earth / Anne Welsbacher.
        p.   cm. — (The universe)
Includes index.
Summary: Discusses our planet's atmosphere, land forms, seasons, weather, life forms, and constantly changing nature.
ISBN 1-56239-720-6
1. Earth—Juvenile literature. [1. Earth.] I. Title. II. Series: Welsbacher, Anne, 1955- Universe.
QB631.4.W45 1997
525—dc20   96-26777
                                                                                      CIP
                                                                                       AC

ABOUT THE AUTHOR
Anne Welsbacher is the director of publications for the Science Museum of Minnesota. She has written and edited science books and articles for children, and has written for national and regional publications on science, the environment, the arts, and other topics.

Contents

The Planet Earth

The Earth is one of nine planets in the **Solar System**. It is the third planet from the Sun and the fifth largest planet. It has one moon.

The Earth is round. It spins on an **axis**, like a top. The top of the Earth is called the **North Pole**. The bottom is the **South Pole**. From the North to the South Pole, the Earth measures 7,900.1 miles (12,713.6 km). The distance through the Earth at the **equator** is 7,926.6 miles (12,756.3 km).

Earth has layers of land, water, and air. These layers support living things. Earth is the only known planet that has life.

North Pole

From top to bottom and side to side, the Earth is nearly the same distance, which makes it round.

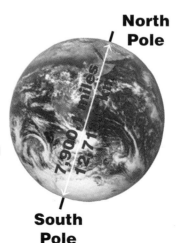

South Pole

4

Six of the nine planets in our Solar System. Earth is seen over the horizon of the Moon, with a Sun flare on the edge.

The Earth's Layers

The solid part of the Earth is called the **lithosphere**. At Earth's center is the core. The core is 2,160 miles (3,480 km) thick and may have two parts: a solid inner core and an outer liquid core.

Around the core is the mantle, which is 1,800 miles (2,900 km) thick. The mantle is solid. But over time the weight of land above it changes its shape.

The crust is the Earth's outer layer. It is 3 to 19 miles (5 to 31 km) thick. The crust slides atop the mantle.

There are many types of rocks in the crust. Some are light while others are heavy. There are also **minerals** such as iron and tin.

Opposite page: A cross-section of Earth showing its different layers.

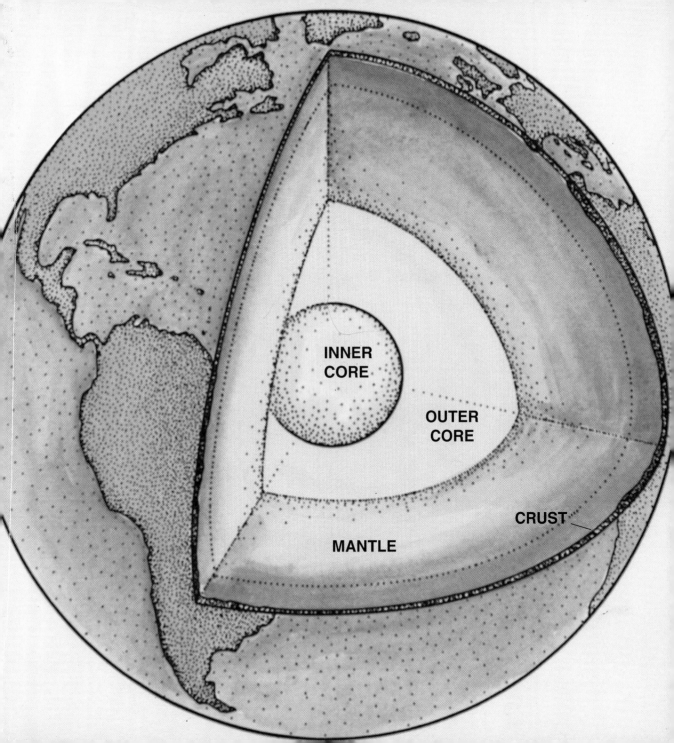

Land Forms

The Earth's crust has seven large chunks of land called **continents**. From largest to smallest, they are Asia, Africa, North America, South America, Antarctica, Europe, and Australia. There are also smaller chunks called islands.

In the central parts of the continents are **plains**. They contain the oldest rocks. Mountains are at the edges of the plains. Other land forms are highlands and lowlands.

Land makes up less than one-third of the planet. Much of the Earth's land is in its northern half.

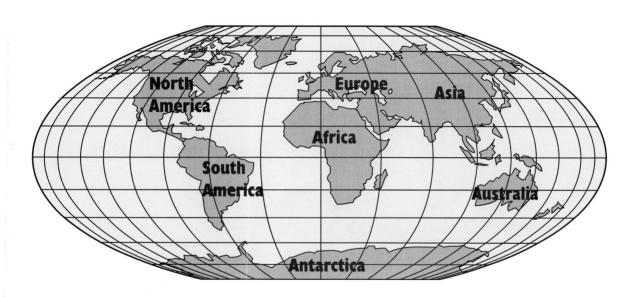

The seven continents of Earth.

The Hydrosphere

The Earth's water is called its **hydrosphere**. Water takes up more than two-thirds of the Earth's surface. It is found in oceans, rivers, streams, lakes, and groundwater. There is also frozen water in mountains, in the Arctic, and in Antarctica.

The Earth's four oceans are the Pacific, the Atlantic, the Indian, and the Arctic. The world's longest river is the Nile, in Africa. The Amazon, in South America, is the second-longest. Other large rivers are the Yangtze (Asia), the Danube (Europe), and the Mississippi (North America).

Water is made up of **hydrogen** and **oxygen**. Water is needed for all life forms. Some living creatures, like humans, need water to drink. Others, like fish, breathe the oxygen in water.

Opposite page: From the Moon the Earth looks blue because of its oceans.

The Atmosphere

The air above the Earth is called the **atmosphere**. The atmosphere is made up of gases and other **elements** like **oxygen.** People need oxygen to breathe.

There are many regions in the atmosphere. The lowest region is the **troposphere**. It is 5 to 10 miles (8 to 16 km) high. All life forms are in the troposphere or in the water below it. The region within the troposphere where life exists is called the **biosphere**. Weather and clouds are also in this region.

Above the troposphere are the **stratosphere**, the **mesosphere**, and the **thermosphere**. In these regions, the air is mostly **nitrogen**. Higher regions are the **exosphere**, the **ionosphere**, and the **magnetosphere**. At these heights are **helium** and **hydrogen** gases.

**Opposite page:
Different regions of the Earth's
atmosphere.**

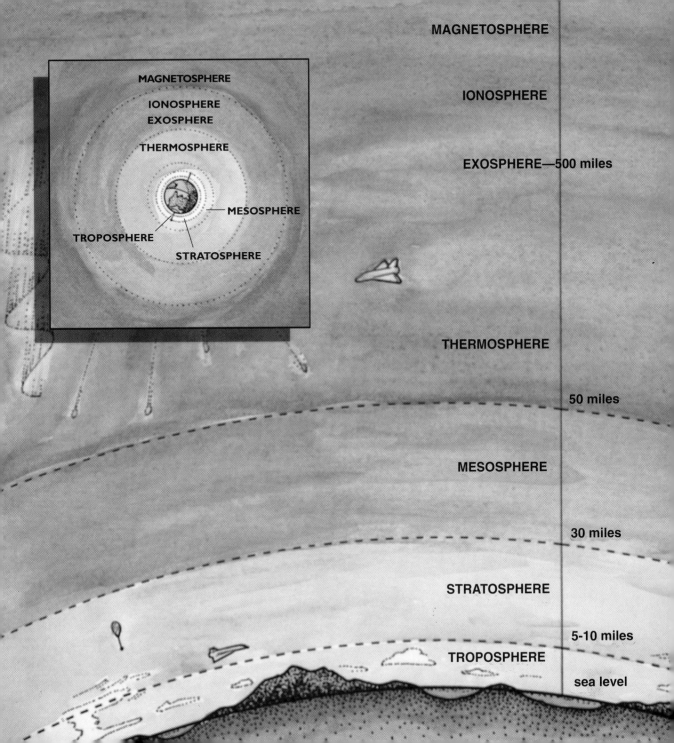

MAGNETOSPHERE

IONOSPHERE

EXOSPHERE—500 miles

THERMOSPHERE

50 miles

MESOSPHERE

30 miles

STRATOSPHERE

5-10 miles

TROPOSPHERE

sea level

MAGNETOSPHERE

IONOSPHERE
EXOSPHERE

THERMOSPHERE

MESOSPHERE

TROPOSPHERE

STRATOSPHERE

Seasons and Weather

The Earth has four seasons: spring, summer, fall, and winter.

The seasons are caused by the tilt of the Earth on its **axis**. When the northern half of the Earth tilts away from the Sun, it is colder in the north and warmer in the south. When the northern half tilts toward the Sun, it is warmer in the north and colder in the south.

The air above the Earth is always moving. Sometimes there is more water in the air. Sometimes it is warm or cold. These and other factors make up the weather.

Opposite page:
The stages of Earth's tilt, which causes the different seasons in the northern and southern half of the planet.

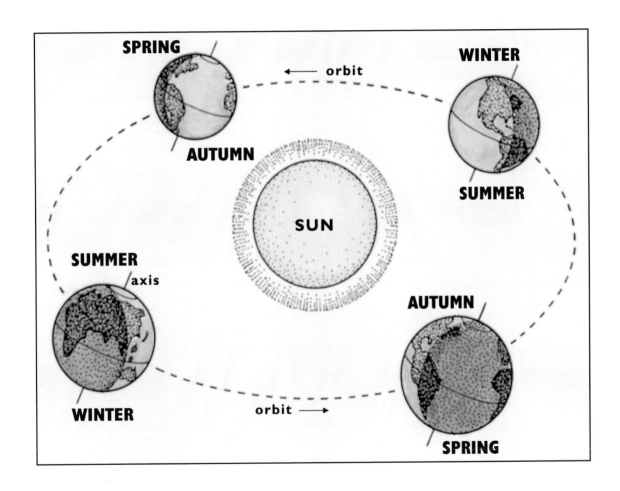

Earth's Plants

Earth is filled with millions of different life forms. Plants are life forms that make their own food and **oxygen**. To do this, they use sunlight, air, and water. This process is called **photosynthesis**.

Trees, ferns, flowers, vines, vegetables, grass, and bushes are plants. All other life forms need these plants to live. Plants create food to eat and oxygen to breathe.

Plants grow almost everywhere on Earth. Trees grow in forests that cover almost one-third of the Earth. Grains grow in open areas called grasslands. Plants also grow in deserts, where there is almost no water. The only places plants do not grow are in the Earth's coldest regions.

Opposite page:
Ground water (1) and nutrients (2) travel through the roots and stems and into the leaves where air (3) is drawn in. Then the plant uses sunlight to change these three elements into food and oxygen.

Photosynthesis

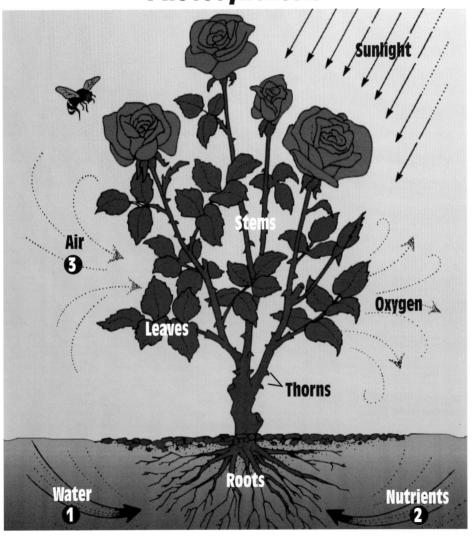

17

Earth's Animals

There are more than a million kinds of animals on Earth, including insects, **reptiles**, birds, and **mammals**.

Animals are found almost everywhere on Earth. They live in the mountains, grasslands, forests, and deserts. They live in cold areas near the North and South Poles.

People are animals, too. People live on only a small part of the planet. Most are in big cities. Few people live in deserts or **polar regions**.

Opposite page:
A group of African lions
basking in the sun.
Animals are found almost
everywhere on Earth.

Our Changing Planet

The Earth is 5 billion years old, and it constantly changes. Wind and water wear down mountains. The Earth's crust moves, causing earthquakes and forming volcanoes. Even the weather changes.

To survive, life must **adapt** to the Earth's changes. Life that cannot adapt dies. Dinosaurs once lived on Earth, but could not adapt to their changing world.

Humans and other living things affect the Earth. We depend on our planet for our food and homes. If we take care of it, it will take care of us.

Glossary

adapt—to change in order to live.

atmosphere (AT-muss-fear)—the air above the Earth.

axis—the imaginary line that goes down the middle of the planet.

biosphere (BYE-us-fear)—region, at or near surface of the Earth, where life exists.

continents (KAHN-tih-nents)—seven large groups of land forming the crust of the Earth; include Asia, Africa, North America, South America, Antarctica, Europe, and Australia.

diversity (duh-VER-suh-tee)—differences among life forms.

element—one of over 100 basic substances from which all other things are made.

equator (e-KWAY-ter)—the imaginary line that goes around the center of the Earth.

exosphere (X-us-fear)—the outermost region of the atmosphere.

helium (HEE-lee-um)—a very light gas that will not burn.

hydrogen (HI-dro-jen)—a colorless gas that burns easily.

hydrosphere (HI-druss-fear)—the Earth's layer of water.

ionosphere (i-ON-us-fear)—the part of the Earth's atmosphere extending from about 30 miles (50km) to the exosphere that contains ionized gases.

lithosphere (LITH-us-fear)—the solid part of the Earth; includes a core, mantle, and crust.

magnetosphere (mag-NET-us-fear)—a region around the Earth in which charged particles are trapped by its magnetic field.

mammals (MAM-ulz)—a group of warm-blooded animals with a backbone and usually having hair.

mesosphere (MEZ-us-fear)—the layer of the atmosphere above the stratosphere.

mineral (MINN-er-ull)—any substance that is not a plant, animal, or another living thing.

nitrogen (NIE-trow-jen)—a gas without color, taste, or smell which forms most of the air.

North Pole—the top of the Earth.

oxygen (OX-uh-jen)—a gas without color, taste, or smell that helps form air and water.

photosynthesis (foe-toe-SIN-thuh-sis)—process used by plants to create food from sun and water.

plains—a flat stretch of land.

polar regions—areas near the North and South Poles.

reptiles—a group of cold-blooded animals that have backbones and are usually covered with scales.

Solar System—The Earth, Moon, planets, and all other heavenly bodies that orbit the Sun.

South Pole—the bottom of the Earth.

stratosphere (STRAT-us-fear)—the nitrogen-rich layer of atmosphere above the troposphere; few clouds form here.

thermosphere (THERM-us-fear)—the layer of atmosphere above the mesosphere which extends into outer space.

troposphere (TROW-puss-fear)—the lowest region of the atmosphere where clouds form.

Earth Facts

Distance From Sun ------ 93 million miles (150 million km)

Diameter ------------------ 7,926 miles (12,760 km)

Age ------------------------- 4.5 to 5 billion years

Most common liquid ---- water

Landforms ---------------- seven continents

Oceans -------------------- four

Temperature high -------- 136° F, Libya

Temperature low --------- minus 128.6° F, Antarctica

Deepest ocean point ---- 36,198 feet (11,033 m), Mariana Trench in the Pacific Ocean

Lowest land point -------- 1,310 feet (399 m) below sea level, Dead Sea shore, Asia

Highest land point ------- 29,028 feet (8,848 m), Mount Everest, Asia

Index